the
BOYs'
BEER
BOOK

"The mouth of a perfectly happy man is filled with beer."

ANCIENT EGYPTIAN PROVERB

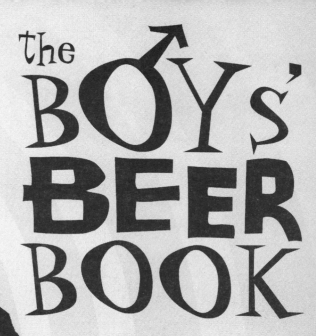

the BOY'S BEER BOOK

BY JONNY GOODALL

ILLUSTRATED BY CARL PEARCE

MITCHELL BEAZLEY

the BOYS' BEER BOOK

BY JONNY GOODALL

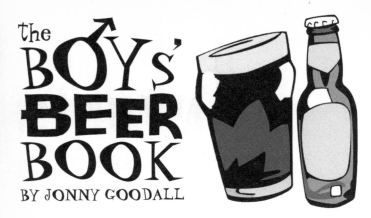

First published in Great Britain in 2004 by Mitchell Beazley, an imprint of Octopus Publishing Group Limited, 2–4 Heron Quays, London E14 4JP.

A CIP catalogue record for this book is available from the British Library.

ISBN: 1-84533-091-9

The author and publishers will be grateful for any information which will assist them in keeping future editions up-to-date. Although all reasonable care has been taken in the preparation of this book, neither the publishers nor the author can accept any liability for any consequences arising from the use thereof, or the information contained therein.

Commissioning Editor
HILARY LUMSDEN

Executive Art Editor
YASIA WILLIAMS-LEEDHAM

Senior Designer
TIM PATTINSON

Managing Editor
JULIE SHEPPARD

Editor
JAMIE AMBROSE

Illustrator
CARL PEARCE

Production
GARY HAYES

Typeset in DaddyO and NoFret

Printed and bound by Mackays Ltd, in the UK

CONTENTS

THE WORLD OF BEER

perfect harmony

Boys & beer in perfect harmony

1.1

"ER, DOS CERVEZAS, MANUEL." "UM, DEUX BIÈRES, MERSEY BOUQUET." THE FIRST FOREIGN PHRASE WE EVER LEARN IS THE DON'T-LEAVE-HOME-WITHOUT-IT NUGGET FOR ORDERING BEER. WE CHOOSE TO MEMORIZE THIS MANTRA EVEN BEFORE WE GET OUR HEADS AROUND EQUALLY USEFUL GEMS LIKE "DOES THIS COME WITH NACHOS?" AND "WHERE'S THE TOILET?" WHAT DOES THIS SAY ABOUT US?

There is certainly a potent alchemy between men and beer.
No one is quite sure how this happy relationship came about,
but I do have my own theories. It is hard to compare the
desperate hordes, or lack of them, outside the toilets in any bar,
pub or club without being reminded of the evolutionary theory
of natural selection. Girls have to wait; boys don't. Beer makes
you pee like a trooper – ergo boys and beer are better suited.
Or perhaps it could simply be that yeast triggers the happy
switch in the "Y" chromosome. I have yet to prove either of
these theories beyond any reasonable doubt, but the simple
deal goes that if boys treat beer right, it will give them a blast.
What goes around comes around.

AND YOU KNOW WHAT? YOU
DON'T NEED TO BECOME A NERD
TO GET INTO BEER. YOU DON'T
HAVE TO GROW A BEARD, GO
UNWASHED, OR SAY GOODBYE
TO YOUR SOCIAL LIFE TO GET
THE BEST OUT OF THE WORLD'S
FAVOURITE DRINK. WELL-MADE,
INTERESTING BEER DOESN'T
BELONG TO THE WEIRDY-
BEARDIES. IT IS TIME TO DRAG

IT, KICKING AND SCREAMING IF NECESSARY, OUT OF THE DINGY, SNUG BAR AND INTO THE LIGHT (NOT TOO MUCH LIGHT, THOUGH, BECAUSE THAT WOULD SPOIL IT).

So when the real-ale brigade starts droning on about what, precisely, is so "real" about cask-conditioned ale, remember that *all* beer is real. What is it you think you're drinking, sunshine? It's all made from the natural, honest-to-goodness ingredients of barley, yeast, water, and hops. What could be simpler than that? Not much – but don't let this lack of pretension put you off from learning just a bit more. You know you're worth it.

From palest El Dorado gold and warmest marmalade hues to the blackness of a panther's pupil; from kicking-back-on-the-river 3 degrees of alcohol to a head-stomping 16 degrees, beer delivers whatever you want it to.

And remember, *you* control the beer – not the other way around. Think of the boy-beer bond as being rather like the symbiotic relationship between the clown fish and the potentially lethal stinging anemone

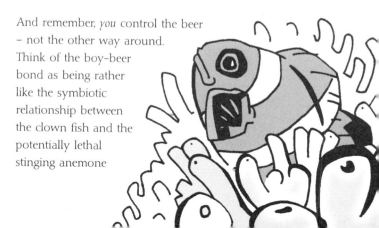

where it chooses to make its home. Treat your beer with respect and you'll get on like fish and chips; diss it, and it'll sting your butt (end of message from our sponsor).

PERHAPS WE STILL ASK FOR JUST "A BEER" BECAUSE WE'RE REASONABLY CONTENT TO SWIG THE UBIQUITOUS, IDENTIKIT MASS-MARKET BRANDS. BUT LOOK AT IT ANOTHER WAY. PERHAPS WE GET WHAT WE DESERVE, AND IF WE UNDERSTOOD A LITTLE MORE ABOUT IT, WE MIGHT START SEEING AN EVEN WIDER CHOICE OF BEER THAN IS ALREADY OUT THERE. THE SADDEST THING ABOUT RESEARCHING THIS BOOK WAS

HOW GODDAMN HARD IT IS TO FIND SOME OF THESE BEERS.

There is undoubtedly a cynical view among some of the suits at the big brewers that we don't drink their beer – we drink their advertising.

But, to quote my favourite beer slogan, from the Wychwood Brewery in Oxfordshire, England, for its dark Hobgoblin ale, ask yourself this question:

"WHAT'S THE MATTER, LAGERBOY: AFRAID YOU MIGHT TASTE SOMETHING?"

Lager lingo ♂

1.2

MEMORIZING HOW TO ORDER A BEER
when you're away from home is right up there with
remembering your ticket, passport, and travellers'
cheques. Even if you've split up with your girlfriend on the
flight, a refreshing beer will always help to refloat your boat.

Wherever you may be, you're more likely to get service with
a smile than a snarl if you can look the waiter in the eye, and
say "Beer" in his language. So on the following pages I've
given the key word for survival in more than fifty countries.
From Azerbaijan to Zaire, you need never just point and
grunt ever again. (You'll have to master "please" and "thank
you" on your own, however. This is a beer book, not a
language course.)

For word nerds, the word "beer" is of Germanic origin, possibly
from the old Teutonic *bewo*, old Saxon *bere* or from the Netherlands,
beura or *bueza*. All are derived from the local word for barley, the
main cereal ingredient.

**PLEASE NOTE: "BIÈRE" IN FRENCH
AND "BIRRA" IN ITALIAN ARE
FEMININE NOUNS. BUT THEN,
SO'S "BEARD" IN FRENCH...**

AFRIKAANS (SOUTH AFRICA)	bier
ALBANIAN	birrë
ARABIC	beereh
AUSTRIAN	Bier
AZERBAIJANI	pivo
BELARUSSIAN	piva
BULGARIAN	bira
CATALAN	cervesa
CHINESE (MANDARIN)	pi jiu
CROATIAN	pivo
CZECH	pivo
DANISH	øl
DUTCH (NETHERLANDS)	bier
ESPERANTO	biero
ESTONIAN	õlu
FINNISH	olut or kalja
FLEMISH	bier
FRENCH	bière
GAELIC (SCOTLAND)	beòir or leann
GERMAN	Bier
GREEK	mpira or tzythos
HAWAIIAN	pia
HEBREW	beera
HUNGARIAN	sör
ICELANDIC	öl or bjór
INDONESIAN	bir
FARSI (IRAN)	ab'jo
IRISH	beoir

ITALIAN	birra
JAPANESE	biiru
KOREAN	mek-ju
LATIN (VATICAN CITY)	cervisia
LATVIAN	alus
LITHUANIAN	alus
MALAY	bir
MANX (ISLE OF MAN)	lhune
MAORI (NEW ZEALAND)	pia
NORWEGIAN	øl
NEPALI	biyar or jad
POLISH	piwo
PORTUGUESE	cerveja
ROMANIAN	bere
RUSSIAN	pivo
SAMI (LAPLAND)	vuola
SERBIAN	pivo
SLOVENIAN	pivo
SPANISH	cerveza
SWAHILI	bia or pombe
SWEDISH	öl
TAGALOG (FILIPINO)	serbesa
THAI	bia
TURKISH	bira
UKRAINIAN	pivo
VIETNAMESE	bia
WELSH	cwrw
ZULU	utshwala

The league of beer-drinkers

1.3

NO BOYS' BOOK WOULD BE COMPLETE WITHOUT A SET OF STATISTICS, so here's the international breakdown of the top beer-drinkers. In the number-one spot is the Czech Republic, birthplace of golden lager; in second place is Ireland, where they're particularly partial to "the black stuff"; and third is Germany, where beer is simply a way of life. No surprises there, then, although beer-guzzling has dipped a little in these countries over the five-year period 1998 to 2002.

AUSTRALIA, NEW ZEALAND AND SOUTH AFRICA – COUNTRIES WHERE BEER-DRINKING IS NEXT TO MANLINESS – CAN HANG THEIR HEADS IN SHAME. BEER HAS EXPERIENCED A SLIGHT DECLINE IN ALL THREE, BUT I GUESS THEY'VE GOT LA-DI-DA WINE NOW.

AS FOR JAPAN, WHERE BEER CONSUMPTION HAS FALLEN BY NEARLY A THIRD: COME ON GUYS! AND BELGIUM, A COUNTRY THAT REGARDS ITSELF AS THE EPICENTRE OF BEER CULTURE, REALLY COULD BE SETTING A BETTER EXAMPLE.

On the way up, the UK has overtaken Denmark to take the number-six spot, while Austria has passed Luxembourg to fourth position.

Spain (up two places to number sixteen), the Slovak Republic, and Italy (both bubbling under at tenth and fortieth, respectively) are traditional wine-drinking countries where younger drinkers are choosing the impossible exoticism of beer – the opposite of what's occurring in Australia, New Zealand, and South Africa.

Russia (up three places to thirty-ninth), and China (up one place to forty-eighth) are putting in stalwart performances, while special mention must go to Thailand, which has shot up an amazing 44.5 per cent and four positions to the number forty-three spot.

WAY TO GO, GUYS!

Beer consumption in litres per head, 1998-2002

(chart position in 1998 in brackets)

		1998	2002	% change
1 (1)	Czech Republic	161.1	155.0	– 3.8
2 (2)	Eire	153.9	147.1	– 4.42
3 (3)	Germany	127.5	121.5	– 4.8
4 (5)	Austria	108.1	109.3	+ 1.1
5 (4)	Luxembourg	110.9	108.2	– 3.0
6 (7)	United Kingdom	99.3	100.6	+ 1.3
7 (6)	Denmark	105.0	96.7	– 8.0
8 (8)	Belgium	98.0	96.0	– 2.1
9 (9)	Australia	94.5	92.4	– 5.0
10 (10)	Slovak Republic	85.2	92.3	+ 8.3
11 (13)	USA	83.7	82.0	– 2.1
15 (11)	New Zealand	84.7	77.8	– 8.2

	1998	2002	% change
16 (18) Spain	66.9	73.4	+ 9.7
20 (17) Canada	68.4	69.9	+2.1
25 (21) South Africa	57.8	55.0	- 4.9
36 (35) France	38.6	34.8	- 9.9
38 (29) Japan	46.3	32.6	- 29.6
39 (42) Russia	26.0	31.1	+ 19.6
40 (40) Italy	26.9	28.2	+ 4.8
43 (47) Thailand	15.5	22.4	+ 44.5
48 (49) China	13.9	16.2	+ 16.5

Source: Commissie Gedistilleerd (published by WARC)

From beer to eternity: a brief history of beer

(with apologies to Stephen Hawking)

4000 BC

The Sumerians produce clay tablets depicting the brewing of beer. Described by Professor Solomon Katz of the University of Pennsylvania as "the world's oldest recipe", this ancient brew is said to have made the drinker feel "exhilarated, wonderful, and blissful". Ninkasi is the Sumerian goddess of brewing.

3000 BC

Stonemasons working on the pyramids are paid in beer, called "kash". It is probably sweetened with dates, aniseed, honey, and saffron. The ancient Egyptian hieroglyph for meal is "beer + bread".

AD 200

The Babylonians plant hops – which begs the question: were these Hanging Hop Gardens of Babylon the eighth wonder of the civilized world?

740

THE GERMANS CATCH ON AND PLANT THEIR OWN HOP GARDENS IN THE HALLERTAU REGION OF BAVARIA. VORSPRUNG HOP TECHNIK, AS THEY SAY IN GERMANY.

1040

The Weihenstephan brewery, the oldest brewery still brewing, is founded near Munich, Germany.

1086

The Domesday Book records forty-three commercial brewers operating in England.

1295

Good King Wenceslas II awards the right to brew to 260 grateful citizens in Pilsen, Bohemia.

1400s

The birth of bottom-fermenting and the first steps towards golden lager (*see* page 32). Brewers in central Europe discover that yeast behaves differently when beer is stored in ice-filled caves – *i.e.* fermentation is much slower...and colder. Pubs are invented in England when women, temporarily, wear the brewing trousers. Most beer at this time is made at home by "ale wives", as it makes perfect sense to brew beer and bake bread at the same time seeing as they contain virtually the same ingredients. The best ale wives put a long pole covered in evergreens (an "ale stake") through their window to attract customers.

1516

Dukes Wilhelm IV and Ludwig X introduce the *Reinheitsgebot*, or "Purity Pledge", in Bavaria, which states that beer must be made only from water, barley malt, yeast, and hops. The rest of Germany adopts the pledge in 1906.

Late 1500s

IN ENGLAND, THE ELIZABETHANS ARE DRINKING MORE BEER THAN WATER. BEER IS SAFER BECAUSE THE WATER IN IT HAS BEEN BOILED. GOOD QUEEN BESS ALLEGEDLY DRINKS A QUART FOR BREAKFAST EVERY DAY – THAT'S TWO PINTS ON THE ROYAL CORNFLAKES EACH MORNING.

1605

The first wheat beer is brewed in Munich, Germany.

1632

The Dutch West India Company opens the first commercial brewery in the USA, in Lower Manhattan, New York. Buffalo, Brooklyn, Albany, and Philadelphia become early brewing centres.

1722

The Bell Brewhouse in Shoreditch, London, makes the first porter: beer made from dark-roasted barley (*see* page 51). Tax on gin (aka "Mother's Ruin") is raised threefold because it's ruining too many mothers. Porter becomes "the universal cordial of the populace".

1759

Arthur Guinness buys a disused brewery in Dublin, Ireland. The rest, appropriately, is history.

1785

British inventor Joseph Bramah patents the beer-pump handle.

1817

Porters and stouts get darker with Daniel Wheeler's patent roasting machine. It's a rotating drum, rather like a coffee roaster, allowing brewers to make black and chocolate malts without burning the barley.

1810

The first year of the Munich Oktoberfest, the world's biggest beer event.

Mid- to late 1800s

Lager brewing goes into overdrive with the help of
refrigeration and ice-making machines developed by Carl
von Linde. Being able to store lager in the brewery sure
beats dragging barrels up into icy mountain caves. Gabriel
Sedlmayr II at Munich's Spaten brewery is the first to
begin lager brewing big-time.

1842

The first golden lager is produced in Pilsen, Bohemia
(*see* page 57). All lagers were dark until this lager landmark.

1859

While playing around with a microscope, Louis Pasteur
unravels the mysteries of yeast. He establishes that it is
not, as is widely believed, something magical and beyond
our control, but a single-cell micro-organism (a fungus, in
fact) that can be manipulated to the benefit of beer.
Unfortunately for purists, he also invents pasteurization,
which some believe makes clean beer at the expense of taste.

Late 1800s

Coinciding with railroads and refrigeration, the second wave
of European settlers, from Germany and Bohemia, spread
their newfangled lagers across America. From breweries in
Cincinnati, St Louis, and Milwaukee, the assault on ales begins.

1876

E. Anheuser and Co. launches US Budweiser.

1883

Scientists achieve the breakthrough in taming yeast, thus removing much of the risk from lager brewing. At the Carlsberg brewery in Copenhagen, Denmark, Emil Hansen discovers how to isolate and cultivate a single-cell, pure-culture lager yeast, classified as *Saccharomyces carlsbergensis*.

1892

Crown caps are invented and the USA sees the patenting of a capping machine capable of sealing 100 bottles per minute. Lager a-go-go.

Early 1900s

Brewers in England start buying their own pubs to create the "tied house" system. The bitter style of beer is invented.

1914-18

The lights go out over Britain as the killjoy Liberal politician, Lloyd George, restricts licensing laws to boost the war effort. The new licensing laws are even worse than those in the Dark Ages (they didn't have licensing laws).

1919-33

ANOTHER INSPIRED PIECE OF LEGISLATION CREATES PROHIBITION AND ORGANIZED CRIME IN THE USA.

1922

Shandy, a mixture of beer and what the Brits call "lemonade"
(sort of like Sprite…) is invented when Bavarian landlord
Franz Xavier Kugler almost runs out of beer. He is credited
with being the first man to dilute it with lemonade.

1927

Colonel Porter invents Newcastle Brown Ale. The next year it
wins first prize for bottled beer at London's Brewers' Exhibition.

1935

Krueger's Finest from New Jersey is the first beer launched
in a can, though you still need a cumbersome device called
a "church key" to open it.

1963

US beer cans are blessed with removable pull tabs. There's
no looking back now.

1971

The Campaign for Real Ale (CAMRA) is launched in England.
This is the start of the revolt against filtered and pasteurized
keg beer by drinkers who pledge their support to cask-
conditioned "real ale". Bearded men tie themselves to pub
barrels in the cellars.

1973

The first Beer Can Regatta is staged in Darwin, Australia.
In 1978, the Can-Tiki (made of 15,000 beer cans) sails
to Singapore.

1976

Inspired by British ales during his military service in Scotland, Jack McAuliffe opens America's first microbrewery in Sonoma, northern California. It closes in 1982, but the torch has been lit. Soon, interesting beers will be made all over the place.

1980

Jonny Goodall gets served his first (legal) pint. "Goodall", incidentally, comes from "good ale".

1985

AMID FEARS OF A SCURVY OUTBREAK, PEOPLE START WEDGING LEMONS IN THEIR BEER BOTTLES. WHEN AN EPIDEMIC FAILS TO MATERIALIZE, THE CRAZE PROVES TO BE SHORT-LIVED.

2004

Andy Fordham (aka The Viking) sets new standards of athletic prowess, winning the Lakeside World Darts Championship. He maintains his performance-enhancing belly by drinking at least fifteen bottles of beer before competing.

BEER CHEMISTRY

Worts & all: how beer is made

2.1

FORGET THOSE HOME-BREWING KITS
you order off the internet (you know the type of thing: just add
water and leave to ferment overnight under the bed). Real men
make real ale, and if you follow these simple instructions you'll
soon know your butt from your hogshead and will be making
world-beating ale of your own. Beer is made from wonderfully
natural ingredients: barley, water, hops, and yeast.

**STEP ONE IS TO FIND YOURSELF
SOME BARLEY, BUT PLEASE
MAKE SURE YOU GET THE
FARMER'S PERMISSION FIRST. I
ALSO ADVISE THAT YOU HAVE
AN ADULT PRESENT AT ALL
TIMES. YOU'LL NEED SHARP
IMPLEMENTS TO CUT OPEN THE
SACKS OF HOPS ("POCKETS")
AND THERE'S SOME HOT
EQUIPMENT TO HANDLE.**

* **Once you've got your barley**, it's time for the three "Ms": malting, milling, and mashing. To convert your barley into malt, steep it in water for a couple of days to encourage germination, then spread it evenly over a large stone floor. Rake it regularly to keep the barley from sticking together and to keep it aerated. Do this for about a week and be careful not to let it sprout. The barley is ready to use when you can munch it like granola.

* **Next, you need to heat your barley** in a kiln. At 60°C (140°F), any germination will be stopped in its tracks. The degree of roasting will affect the style of your finished beer, as will the type of cereal used. Lightly roasted barley, known as white malt, is ideal for making lager; heavily roasted, dark malts are great for making porters and stouts, while something in the middle is good for ale.

MALTED BARLEY PRODUCES SOFT, SWEETISH, CLEAN FLAVOURS, WHILE WHEAT MAKES SHARPER, TARTER BEER. CORN AND RICE, USED WIDELY IN THE USA, MAKE LIGHTER-BODIED AND

LIGHTER-TASTING BEER.
WE'RE MAKING A
TRADITIONAL ALE HERE,
SO I'LL ASSUME YOU'VE
MADE MEDIUM-ROASTED
BARLEY MALT.

* **Next up, grind you malt** in a mill to make a fine mixture of flour and husks called "grist". Watch your fingers.

* **Chuck the grist in a large container** ("mash tun") and get ready to do the monster mash. Mix it with hot water (about 65°C/149°F) and leave it to stand for one or two hours. This releases the barley's sugars for fermenting. You'll need hard water with plenty of mineral salts to make ale. And you'll be needing lots of it – even the strongest beer is ninety per cent water. Incidentally, brewers are now able to treat waters to the extent that they can make any style of beer pretty much anywhere.

* **You should now have a clear, watery solution** called "wort" (pronounced *wurt*, if you really want to impress). Run this off into a large copper vessel and bring to the boil

for up to an hour and a half. If you're short of cash, you might want to sell the "spent grains" (the sludge left behind in the mash tun) for animal feed.

* **While the mash is boiling**, throw in your hops, keeping a few handfuls back for later. At this stage of the brewing process they will add dryness and bitterness to balance out the biscuity sweetness of your malt. They will also prevent bacterial infections. Other traditional plants and herbs you might want to add include rosemary, rosehips, ginger, licorice, ginger, thistles – and, of course, bog myrtle.

* **Now you're ready** to start fermenting. Allow your wort to cool to about 18°C (64°F) and transfer it to a large, open, wooden fermenting vessel. At this stage, add (or "pitch in") your yeast. Yeast is a microscopic member of the fungus family. It consumes sugar to produce alcohol (hooray!) and carbon dioxide (fizz) in the process of fermentation. It is the greatest single influence on the flavour of beer and why brewers store their irreplaceable yeast strains in high-security "yeast banks".

YOUR BREW SHOULD BE
BUBBLING AWAY NICELY NOW,
PRODUCING A **THICK BLANKET**
OF **FOAM** ON THE SURFACE
AND REACHING A **TEMPERATURE**
OF ABOUT 25°C (77°F). THERE
ARE **TWO BASIC** STYLES OF
BREWER'S YEAST: **ALE AND
LAGER** (*SEE* **OVERLEAF**). YOU
WILL BE NEEDING AN ALE
YEAST, BUT **EVEN HERE**,
THERE ARE MANY TO
CHOOSE FROM, ACCORDING
TO THE **SPECIFIC STYLE**
YOU WANT TO MAKE.
WHEN THE **YEAST HAS**
GORGED ITSELF ON

THE SUGARS, IT BECOMES INACTIVE AND THE FERMENTATION IS COMPLETE.

Let it cool, then pour it into barrels. To condition it, add a touch more yeast and a sprinkling of sugar to cause a secondary fermentation and a little more fizz. To clarify your beer, add some "isinglass finings" (ask a grown-up). These will attract the yeast cells, causing them to clump together and sink to the bottom of the cask. You might wish to boost your beer's hoppy, floral aromas at this stage by throwing in a few more handfuls of hops (this is called "dry hopping").

So there you have it. The basis for brewing beer is to turn barley into malt, extract its sugars, boil it with hops, and ferment it with yeast.

CONGRATULATIONS! YOU'VE JUST MADE YOUR OWN ALE!!

SIMPLY DISTIL YOUR BEER TO MAKE WHISK(E)Y.

ale vs Lager:

Top-fermenting vs bottom-fermenting beers

THERE ARE A NUMBER OF DIFFERENCES between ale and lager brewing, but the most significant is that ale is "top-fermenting" while lager is "bottom-fermenting". It's very easy to remember, because bottom-fermenting for lager produces the gassier styles of beer (and if you can't appreciate the puerile connection between bottom-fermenting and gas, then frankly you're reading the wrong beer book).

During fermentation, top-fermenting ale yeasts rise to the top of the tank, attacking the sugars and producing an enormous amount of foam, heat, and fury. Lager yeasts, in contrast, sink to the bottom of the tank where they slowly nibble away at the sugars at near-freezing temperatures. This is why top-fermenting and bottom-fermenting are also known as warm- and cold-fermenting, respectively.

TOP-FERMENTING ALES ARE ROUNDER, FRUITIER, AND MORE COMPLEX, WHILE BOTTOM-FERMENTING LAGERS ARE MORE REFRESHING, CRISPER, AND CLEANER.

By the way, "lager" is actually taken from a verb in German: "lagern" meaning "to store". In the days before refrigeration, the brewers of Bavaria would store, or lagern, their beers in icy caves in the Alps to keep them fresh for summer drinking. This is how bottom-fermenting lager yeasts were cultivated and then mastered. So now you know.

Hip hops

2.2

YOU WON'T FIND CANNABIS IN A CAN-A-BEER, but, if you're lucky, you might find something quite similar. The hop, which is closely related to both the nettle and "the weed", is one of beer's primary ingredients. Its Latin name is *Humulus lupulus* (wolf plant) because, if left unchecked, it will spread voraciously through fields and hedges, choking other plants as it goes.

BEER IS NOT "MADE FROM HOPS", AS SOME BELIEVE. BEER IS MADE FROM BARLEY, YEAST, AND WATER, WITH HOPS PROVIDING THE SEASONING. TYPICALLY, A BARREL OF BEER IS MADE FROM 20KG (44LBS) OF MALT TO 150G (5.50Z) OF HOPS. THINK OF HOPS AS THE SALT ON YOUR PRETZELS, THE SOY SAUCE IN YOUR STIR-FRY.

Malty brews will always tend towards the sweet and biscuity without the balancing act of fruit, herbs, and spices. Juniper berries, orange peel, rosehips, ginger, and rosemary have all been used at one time or another to give beer that certain *je ne sais quoi*. And who can forget the charms of bog myrtle?

TODAY, HOWEVER, HOPS ARE THE BREWER'S CHOICE, AND THIS PROBABLY HAS AS MUCH TO DO WITH THEIR NATURAL PRESERVATIVE QUALITIES AS THE PLEASANTLY BITTER AND AROMATIC NUANCES THEY GIVE TO BEER. HOP CONES, THE BLOSSOM OF THE HOP PLANT, ARE RICH IN RESINS AND ESSENTIAL OILS, WHICH IMPART SPICY, FLORAL, RESINOUS, AND CITRIC CHARACTERS, ACCORDING TO THE VARIETY USED.

Hops impart different qualities to beer, depending on the stage of the brewing process at which they're added. If they're introduced early on, when the malt and water are boiling in the brew-kettle, hops add dryness and bitterness. Added late in the boil ("late-hopping"), they contribute a range of spicy and citric flavours and aromas. Traditional British cask ales are often "dry-hopped", which means more hops are added to the barrels of beer right at the end, and this can make for quite a heady, hoppy perfume in the finished beer.

THE MAGNIFICENTLY NAMED GOLDING AND FUGGLE ARE THE CLASSIC ENGLISH HOP VARIETIES, GROWN MAINLY IN THE COUNTIES OF KENT AND HEREFORD. BROADLY SPEAKING, **THE EARTHY, GRASSY FUGGLE IS USED FOR BITTERING, WHILE THE CITRIC, FLORAL GOLDING IS USED FOR** AROMA, OCCASIONALLY ADDING **A RICH, MARMALADE QUALITY** TO ENGLISH ALES.

In the USA, the main areas of hop-growing are the Yakima Valley in Washington State, the Willamette Valley in Oregon, and the Snake River Valley in Idaho. The Cluster is the principal bittering hop, while Cascade adds buckets of aroma. American hops can be quite aggressively resiny, citric, and floral, sometimes packing a powerful, grapefruity punch.

THE CLASSIC LAGER VARIETIES ARE THE DELICATELY FLORAL AND AROMATIC SAAZ HOP, GROWN AROUND THE TOWN OF ZATEC IN THE CZECH REPUBLIC (IT'S USED TO MAKE THE ORIGINAL GOLDEN PILSNER), AND THE EQUALLY SUBTLE AND PERFUMED HALLERTAU MITTELFRÜH VARIETY FROM THE HALLERTAU DISTRICT OF BAVARIA, NEAR MUNICH.

Hops contain potent antioxidants which can help combat cholesterol. In the olden days, they were used to treat migraines, bed-wetting, and leprosy, which is handy. Stuffed into pillows, hops fight insomnia. They were also once thought of as an aphrodisiac, which strikes me as a bit of a contradiction.

Beer, there, & everywhere: the styles of beer

THERE ARE MORE STYLES OF BEER than even a tanked–up Aussie could shake a six-pack at. For this reason, you'll be relieved to hear that most of these styles fall into one of two categories: ale, which is top-fermented, and lager, which is bottom-fermented (*see* pages 42–45). All the classic beer styles originate from northern, central, and eastern Europe; ale comes from the north (Britain), and lager from the centre (Germany) and east (Bohemia, today's Czech Republic). Lager has gradually spread to all corners of the globe, while ale, in its few outposts, has generally been considered a quirky little brew for isolated pockets of eccentrics. But this attitude has been changing in recent years, due mainly to a growing band of brothers setting up microbreweries, notably in the USA and UK, with the express purpose of reviving "lost" ale (and lager) recipes. These have generally bypassed the multinational brewers, but some of the larger, regional breweries have joined this revivalist trend, dipping their toes into styles of beer they had long considered painfully unfashionable. As we speak, the classic beer styles are being refashioned and reinterpreted wherever men dare to dream – and to drink.

HERE THEY ARE, IN ALL THEIR GLORY...

Ales

ENGLISH ALES INCLUDE MILD,
BITTER, PALE ALE, BROWN ALE,
OLD ALE, INDIA PALE ALE (IPA),
AND BARLEY WINE. THEY ARE
ALL LOW IN THE FIZZ FACTOR
COMPARED TO LAGER, AND RANGE
IN STRENGTH FROM MILD, AT
ABOUT 3 DEGREES OF ALCOHOL,
UP TO BARLEY WINE
AT A MASSIVE
11 DEGREES
OR SO. MOST,
HOWEVER, ARE
BETWEEN 3
AND 4 DEGREES.

Bitter

Bitter is usually served on tap in pubs and is the most popular style of ale in England.

IT'S DRY YET FRUITY WITH A PLEASANTLY BITTERSWEET TANG: THE RESULT OF ENORMOUS AMOUNTS OF HOPS; FUGGLES AND GOLDINGS ARE THE CLASSIC VARIETIES USED. QUAFFING BITTERS COME IN AT AROUND 3 TO 4 DEGREES OF ALCOHOL, WITH "BEST" OR "SPECIAL" BITTERS AROUND 4 TO 5 DEGREES.

Mild

Mild is generally dark-brown beer, low in alcohol (3 to 3.8 degrees), though it is often quite full-bodied. "Mild" refers to the fact that these beers are lightly hopped. Relatively sweet and malty, mild ales suffer from a bit of a blue-collar image, as they were originally made for swilling by thirsty factory workers.

Pale ale

The less bitter, maltier forefather of bitter, created in the
English ale capital of Burton-on-Trent. It can be quite citric
on the palate, with nutty, biscuity tones. Pale ale is not
especially pale, but was given its name to differentiate
it from the likes of porter and stout.

India pale ale (IPA)

IPA is a supercharged pale ale that can reach 5 degrees
of alcohol plus. This perfumed, hop-packed, floral style
is so named because it was originally brewed for Brits in
India. The preservative qualities of hops, combined with
the relatively high level of alcohol, helped to keep it in
good condition on its long voyage. IPAs are enjoying
something of a resurgence in the USA, thanks to hop-
handed microbrewers.

Brown ale

The macho beer of the north of England. It's amber-brown
in colour with a light, hoppy aroma, malty palate, occasional
hints of chocolate or coffee, and an invariably dry finish.
Most are about 4.5 to 5 degrees of alcohol. Southern
English examples tend to be sweeter and lower in alcohol.

Old ale

is full of it: colour, body, and flavour, and is usually quite
hefty in the alcohol stakes at around six per cent. Old ales
are rich, dark, and sweet with raisins and molasses on the
palate. Great for warming vital organs in winter.

Barley wine

Barley wine is usually served in small "nip" bottles as it
packs an even bigger punch than old ale, starting at around
6 degrees of alcohol and scaling the dizzy heights of
12 degrees – the strength of many wines. Sometimes known
as "stingo", it is copper to mahogany in colour with a fairly
sweet palate of raisins and coffee. Barley wine makes a superb
winter warmer and can also be served as a dessert beer.

Real ale

So what's this "real ale" thing the
British and other fanatical beer buffs
keep talking about? Basically, it refers
to cask-conditioned ales, which means
the ales leave the brewery in cask in an
unfinished state and continue to improve
via a secondary fermentation that takes
place in the pub cellar. The beer is neither
filtered nor pasteurized, so it has a relatively
short shelf-life, which is why real ales are
found only in dedicated pubs. As it matures,
the beer gains slightly in strength and fruitiness.
The Brits drink their beer "warm" because if real ale is chilled
it simply doesn't work.

Nitro-keg beer, which has been pasteurized and pepped up
with nitrogen to give it extra creaminess, is the antithesis of
real ale. Unfortunately, the big brewers are generally keener
to market nitro-beer because of its substantially longer
shelf-life – and, paradoxically, greater profitability.

Scottish ale

Scottish ale reflects the Scottish climate. Hops, which don't grow in Scotland, are used very sparingly, so the emphasis is on rich maltiness. Dark and full-bodied, Scottish ales are comforting to drink in the Scottish winter – and summer, come to think of it. They range in strength from 3 degrees of alcohol to a mighty 10 degrees, and are described, in ascending order, as "light", "heavy", "export", and, endearingly, "wee heavy".

Porter & stout

Made from heavily roasted barley, these are the roasty, toasty, heavily hopped, black beers.

PACKED WITH COFFEE AND BITTER-CHOCOLATE FLAVOURS, THAT ARE ALMOST MEALS IN THEMSELVES. THE FIRST BEER TO BE BREWED ON AN INDUSTRIAL SCALE, PORTER POWERED LONDON'S WORKFORCE DURING THE INDUSTRIAL REVOLUTION, WHEN IT WAS PARTICULARLY POPULAR AMONG THE PORTERS OF LONDON'S MARKETS.

TODAY, DRY STOUT IS STRONGLY LINKED WITH IRELAND AND OYSTERS. AS ITS NAME SUGGESTS, STOUT, AT AROUND 5.7 DEGREES OF ALCOHOL, TENDS TO BE THE FULLER-BODIED AND STRONGER OF THE TWO STYLES.

PORTERS AND STOUTS ARE ENJOYING A RENAISSANCE IN THE USA AND HAVE ENTHUSIASTIC FOLLOWERS IN PARTS OF AFRICA AND THE WEST INDIES, WHERE THEIR IRON CONTENT IS THOUGHT TO, ER, "PUT LEAD IN ONE'S PENCIL".

VARIATIONS INCLUDE LOW-ALCOHOL MILK STOUT (3 TO 3.5 DEGREES), WHICH

CONTAINS MILK SUGARS, IS LESS GASSY (NICER FOR THE LADIES), AND IS PROMOTED AS A PICK-ME-UP; SMOOTH OATMEAL STOUT, WITH ADDED OATMEAL; AND OYSTER STOUT, WHICH CONTAINS GRANULATED EXTRACT OF OYSTERS.

ORIGINALLY MADE FOR EXPORT TO RUSSIA, IMPERIAL STOUT IS THE TARRY, TREACLY MOTHER OF ALL STOUTS AT A WHOPPING 7 TO 10 DEGREES OF ALCOHOL.

Wheat beer

The "bubblegum" beer of Bavaria and Berlin is an acquired taste which, I admit, I have only just acquired. It is, however, massively popular among those "who dare to be different". Made with varying proportions of wheat and barley, these are pale, cloudy, refreshing beers with a tart, fruity taste, often with pronounced flavours of banana, cloves, coriander, and, yes, bubblegum. *Berliner Weisse*, or "white" beer, is super-thirst-quenching, low in alcohol (around 3 degrees), and so sharp that the locals often drink it with an alleviating dash of raspberry or other fruit syrup. In southern Germany, *Weizen* ("wheat" beer), is generally less aggressive and hovers around 5 degrees. The Bavarians also make dark wheat beers (*Dunkel Weizen*) and supercharged wheat bears (*Weizenbock*).

Kölsch

The golden beer of Cologne, or Koln as it's called in Germany. It might look as pale as lager but it packs the fruitiness of an ale. Highly quaffable and perfumed with hops, *Kölsch* is around 4.3 to 5 degrees of alcohol. It is said to be good for the digestion – which is handy, really, as it's often served with the local blood sausage called *Kölsch* caviar. It is served in tall, slender glasses (*Stangen*) from huge, round trays by waiters referred to as *Köbes*, short for *Jakob*.

Alt

Alt means "old" and is the descriptor for the amber and copper-coloured beers from downtown Düsseldorf.

WITH THEIR HOPPY OVERTONES, SWEET MALTINESS, AND BISCUITY RICHNESS, THEY BEAR COMPARISON WITH THE ALES OF ENGLAND. THEIR

STRENGTH RANGES FROM 4.5 TO 4.7 DEGREES OF ALCOHOL. GREAT WITH OFFAL OR A NICE SALTED PIG'S TROTTER – MMMM...

Bière de garde

Means "keeping beer" because, traditionally, it was laid down for drinking in the summer months. For this reason, *biere de garde* is often put in Champagne-style bottles. This sweetly malty style, with a good dose of spicy hops and sherry-like fruit, is making a bit of a comeback among the growing number of microbreweries in the Nord-Pas de Calais region along the border with France's beery neighbours in Belgium. *Bières de gardes* are fairly strong, ranging from 4.4 to 7.5 degrees. Traditionally, they were all top-fermented like an ale, but there has been a creeping tendency to bottom-ferment and filter them. *Bière de garde* is said to be tasty with the local *andouillettes* (tripe sausages). Hold me back…

Trappist Ales

Ending our ale section on a religious note –

THESE MIGHTY POTENT (6 TO 12 DEGREES OF ALCOHOL) BOTTLED BEERS ARE BREWED BY THE TRAPPIST MONKS IN ONLY FIVE

BELGIAN ABBEYS - CHIMAY, ORVAL, ROCHEFORT, WESTMALLE, SAINT SIXTUS - AND ONE IN THE NETHERLANDS CALLED SCHAAPSKOOI. THESE ARE MOSTLY RICH, SWEET, HEADY BREWS WITH HINTS OF FRUITCAKE BALANCED BY INTENSE, HOPPY BITTERNESS. THE BROTHERS DRINK THEIR BEERS, OFTEN REFERRED TO AS "LIQUID BREAD", TO FUEL THEM THROUGH LENT - WHICH, BY THE WAY, IS WHY THEY HAVE PERFECTED A HAND SIGNAL TO SILENTLY ENQUIRE "IS IT LENT YET?"

Lagers

Pilsner

Like silence, pilsner is golden. The
beautiful brew of Bohemia (today's
Czech Republic) was created in 1842
in the city of Pilsen, when the first
beer resembling what we would
recognize as lager was produced by
the method of bottom-fermentation
(*see* pages 39–40).

Up until this point all beers were
dark or cloudy (or both) and
this new style rapidly caught on,
coinciding, as it did, with the wider adoption of glass
drinking vessels, replacing wood and metal. This was
an exciting time. The first pilsner was brewed from
barley grown in Bohemia and neighbouring Moravia
and aromatized with the local Saaz hop. The brewery that
blew the beer world's doors open still operates and sells
its beers under the Pilsner Urquell brand. The Urquell bit,
which means "original source", was added in 1898, but
it was too late to prevent the widespread imitation of this
ground-breaking style.

The Gambrinus Brewery, adjacent to the Pilsner Urquell
Brewery, also makes beer that can justifiably call itself
pilsner (meaning "from Pilsen").

SOON AFTER THE BREWERS OF PILSEN STRUCK LIQUID GOLD, THE BOHEMIAN CITY OF CESKE BUDEJOVICE (KNOWN IN GERMANY AS BUDWEIS) CAME UP WITH ITS OWN GOLDEN INTERPRETATION. THESE ARE THE GENUINE PILSNERS, THOUGH BREWERS THROUGHOUT THE WORLD FLATTER THROUGH IMITATION. IN GERMANY, THIS STYLE IS CALLED PILSNER, SOMETIMES ABBREVIATED TO PILS.

A "PROPER" PILSNER SHOULD HAVE PLENTY OF FLOWERY, SPICY, HOP AROMA WITH RIPE MALT AND A TOUCH OF ROASTED GRAIN ON THE

PALATE. IT SHOULD HAVE A DRY FINISH, A FINE FOAM, AND ABOUT 5 DEGREES OF ALCOHOL. THE CITY OF PILSEN, INCIDENTALLY, IS ALSO THE BIRTHPLACE OF THE SKODA AUTOMOBILE.

Helles

Helles is a light, golden quaffing beer from Bavaria with about 4.6 degrees of alcohol. Classic examples boast plenty of malt and floral hop character with delicate, citric fruit on the palate. Like all German beer, it clings proudly to the sixteenth-century *Reinheitsgebot* ("Pure Beer Pledge"), which states that German beer can be made only from malted barley, wheat, hops, yeast, and water. No other additives or adjuncts (cheap, unmalted cereals) are permitted. All a bit paranoid, if you ask me.

Dunkel

Dunkel is, intriguingly, a dark lager from Munich. Predating the golden Pilsner revolution, the best of these beers combine the sweet, nutty maltiness of ale with the cleanness of lager. They are usually around 4.8 degrees of alcohol.

Marzen & Oktoberfestbier

Sweetish, spicy, amber-red lagers are traditionally served
at Munich's legendary Oktoberfest. In the days before
refrigeration they were brewed in March (März in German)
and stored through the summer for autumn/winter drinking.
They range from 5 to 6 degrees of alcohol and are great
with oriental-style food. The malt is kilned to an amber tone,
which some brewers still call "Vienna malt" in reference
to the off-dry, reddish lagers once brewed in that austrian city.
This style is being adopted by a number of US microbreweries.

Bock

The German name for strong lagers ranging from 6 to 8
degrees of alcohol. It also means "goat", a head-banging
little critter that is depicted on many *Bock* labels. The name,
however, comes from a corruption of Einbeck, the town near
Hanover where this style originated.
These are usually quite sweet and
malty, with dark fruit and spicy hops,
though they vary in colour through
golden, tawny, and deep brown.
Extra-strong bocks, which can scale the
giddy heights of 14 degrees of alcohol,
are known as *Doppelbocks* or *Starkbier*
(strong beer). They tend to have names like
Celebrator, Triumphator, and Maximator,
though I have yet to find one called
Terminator. In an *Eisbock*, the concentration
is hiked up through freezing – the water
freezes at a lower temperature than the
alcohol, and then the ice is removed.

Speciality beers

Lambic beer

Most beer is made using cultivated yeasts which brewers keep protected in "yeast banks". The lambic beers of the Senne Valley in Belgium, however, are the result of airborne wild yeasts having their wicked way with the fermenting brew. Those who make these feral beers are careful to leave their windows open to invite the wild yeasts in, and they are very reluctant to disturb the dust and cobwebs in their cellars for fear of removing the unique yeasts that live there. This is the way all beers used to be made. Wild yeasts impart winey, cidery, sherry-like qualities to the beer, which is generally refreshingly tart and quite still. Lambic beers contain at least thirty per cent wheat and weigh in at around 4.5 to 5 degrees of alcohol. They take their name from the town of Lembeek.

Gueuze

Pronounced *gerser*, this is a blend of young and mature lambic beers. The young beers prompt a secondary fermentation in the bottle, producing a sparkling beer which many consider to be the Champagne of the beer world. The bottles are sealed with Champagne-style corks and are laid down to mature for six to eighteen months.

GUEUZE IS QUITE ACIDIC, CIDERY, AND REFRESHING BUT SLIGHTLY STRONGER THAN

STANDARD LAMBIC BEER, REACHING AROUND 5.5 DEGREES OF ALCOHOL.

Fruit beers

Long before hops were added to beer for their bitterness and preservative qualities, brewers would use various fruits, herbs, and spices to give a little edge to their malt-heavy beer. Brewers in the Low Countries of Northern Europe took a particular shine to cherries and raspberries, using them to make *Kriek* (cherry beer) and **Frambozen** (raspberry beer). These are, surprisingly, deliciously refreshing with a sweet-sour palate and a dry finish. Alcohol ranges from 5 to 6 degrees.

Steam beer

A unique style, the name of which is protected by the Anchor Steam Beer brewery of San Francisco. It's an ale-lager lovechild made with bottom-fermenting lager yeast but fermented at an ale temperature. This is achieved by fermenting the beer in very shallow tanks, only two-feet (0.7-metres) deep.

The beer undergoes a second fermentation in cask that is so vigorous the escaping gas is said to sound like steam. The finished beer, at around 5 degrees of alcohol, is pretty fizzy. Rather like German *Dunkel* beer, steam beer unites the fruitiness of ale with the cleanness of lager.

Adelaide sparkling ale

There is an oasis of ale-brewing even in the dyed-in-the-wool lagerland of Australia. Cooper's Sparkling Ale, the originator of the style, is sparkling in the fizzy sense, but not visually. Sharp and spritzy on the palate, it is surprisingly cloudy on the eye.

Chocolate beer

By roasting dark, malted barley to a specific degree, brewers are able to produce "chocolate malt" which imparts attractive chocolaty flavours. In recent years some have even added chocolate essence or cocoa powder. The ones I have tasted have managed to retain a pleasingly dry finish.

IF THIS IS AN ATTEMPT TO WOO FEMALE DRINKERS, WHY NOT JUST PUT A PICTURE OF BRAD PITT STROKING A KITTEN ON THE LABEL?

RIGHT BEER, RIGHT NOW

Right beer, right glass: serving, tasting, & appreciating beer

3.1

MARKETING MEN HAVE SPENT MILLIONS perfecting the glasses to best present their beloved brands. Curves and contours fit the drinker's hand so that the embossed logo isn't obscured. Most of these designs are very effective on an aesthetic level, and the "theatre" of ordering a beer is greatly enhanced. When it comes to fully appreciating the aromas and flavours of beer, however, there is no better design than a large wine glass. Oh, the bitter irony...

TO GET THE **BEST** FROM ANY DRINK – WINE, WHISK(E)y, RUM, BEER – yOU NEED TO BE ABLE TO SWIRL IT ROUND THE GLASS TO RELEASE ITS AROMAS BEFORE PLUNGING yOUR NOSE IN AND SNIFFING DEEPLY.

TRY SWIRLING A LARGE COLD ONE IN A BUSY BAR WITHOUT SOAKING A THREE-FOOT (C. 1-METRE) RADIUS. NOT ADVISED.

While your tongue can detect only four sensations – saltiness, bitterness, sweetness, and sourness – your nose can smell thousands of aromas. But can you describe them? Your motive for wanting to describe your beer might stem from a genuine desire to record your favourite brands and styles, or it might arise from a more primeval urge to stand at the bar pontificating like a ponce. Maybe it's a bit of both.

BUT WHICH WORDS TO USE? IF YOU STICK YOUR NOSE IN YOUR GLASS AND YOU GET **LOADS OF TOADS**, SAY SO; OR IF YOU'RE REMINDED OF A **BADGER** IN DAMP **UNDERPANTS**, YOU REALLY SHOULD SPEAK OUT.

To make all this much easier, a bunch of beardy beer boffins got together back in the '70s at the Brewing Research Foundation in Surrey, England, to invent the wheel – the "Beer Flavour Wheel", to be precise. It looks like one of those "cake" pieces in Trivial Pursuit, divided into technicolour segments, each describing various aromas and flavours as well as the way the beer actually feels in your mouth ("mouth-feel").

These adjectives have become the standard currency, internationally, for describing beer, and in "The language of love" (see page 79) I've selected what I consider some of the most useful.

ONCE YOU'VE ASSESSED THE AROMAS AND FLAVOURS OF YOUR BEER (THE SMELL USUALLY INDICATES WHAT TASTES YOU CAN EXPECT), CONSIDER ITS MOUTH-FEEL. IS IT LIGHT-BODIED OR FULL-BODIED? DOES IT SLIDE OVER YOUR TONGUE LIKE A SILK SCARF, OR IS IT A BIT

"CHEWY"? AND FINALLY, TRY TO GAUGE ITS FINISH. IS IT DRY AND BITTER, SWEET AND MALTY, FRESH AND HOPPY OR A MIXTURE OF ALL? HAVE YOU FORGOTTEN ITS FLAVOUR ALREADY, OR DOES IT GO ON FOREVER, STRETCHING SENSUALLY TOWARDS A HORIZON OF PURE HEDONISM?

The colour of beer is decided by the type of barley used and the kilning time and temperature during the malting process (*see* pages 32–38). Pale, quick-dried malts, for example, make lighter styles like *Kölsch* and *Helles*, while dark, roasted malts are used to make stouts and porters.

Serve it right

Beer's greatest enemies are heat, light, and detergent, not necessarily in that order. Let's get the serving temperature right first. It's a myth, perpetrated by sore rugby losers, that the Brits drink warm beer. For best results, ales should be served chilled at 11-12°C (52-54°F), which takes about two hours in the fridge. Lager should be cold, at around 6-8°C (46-48°F), which, in fridge terms, usually involves an overnight stay. The only beers that benefit from being served at room temperature are strong barley wines, old ales, and Christmas ales, which deserve this respect owing to their spicy, complex, (some might say vinous) aromas and flavours.

Incidentally, the old-fashioned ale jug is designed with a handle so you can pick it up without your clammy hands touching – and warming – the glass. By far the most important thing about glassware for beer is that it's squeaky clean. The smallest trace of detergent will destroy the foaming head on any beer, so be warned. There are tiny pits in the surface of a glass which serve to produce a stream of bubbles to replenish the head. If these are clogged with soap, you can kiss your head goodbye.

Get a head

Few issues obsess even the most casual drinker as much as the head on a beer. In fact, there have probably been more beer-related murders over this single issue than any other, yet many of the arguments are so much twaddle. I've even heard it suggested that the head on a beer keeps it fresh and prevents bubbles from escaping. Rubbish. How much freshness can a beer lose over the twenty minutes it takes to drink it? The head, or foam, is produced by proteins in the malted barley; bitterness from the hops helps both to stabilize it and to make it stick to the sides of the glass as it's drunk. This produces the "lacing" effect (rings of foam) that seems so important to beer-drinkers in the north of England.

AN EMINENT BEER BOFFIN HAS CONVINCED ME THAT THE HEAD IS LITTLE MORE THAN AN AESTHETIC CONSIDERATION. "IT'S A TEXTURAL THING," HE EXPLAINED. "IT'S NICE TO DRINK BEER THROUGH BUBBLES AND IT JUST MAKES IT LOOK SO MUCH BETTER."

But, assuming the foam on your beer is important to you, here is some excellent advice on how to keep your head while those around you are losing theirs. For example, if you stick your finger into a frothing beer – perhaps, say, to remove a fly – traces of oil from your skin are enough to make the head vanish. Similarly, the foam will break down if you eat a fatty snack, like a packet of peanuts, when your lips come into contact with the beer.

I'd also like to explode the myth that lipstick is good for a foaming, frothing head. It has the same effect as fatty food on the lips and makes the foam disappear. Try these amazing tricks in the pub to thrill your friends. Go easy on the lipstick. You shouldn't really have much more than one centimetre (half an inch) of foam on a glass of beer, and you should take it back if you feel you've been short-changed. We all know that continental types serve beer so frothy that chocolate syrup and a cherry wouldn't look out of place on it, but most of the head is above the rim of the glass, so it shouldn't be a problem for you.

And don't let anyone tell you that traditional, cask-conditioned ale shouldn't have a head, because it should. If yours hasn't got one, it means it hasn't been stored or served properly. It should never resemble the Continental ice-cream effect, but there should be a discernible head nonetheless.

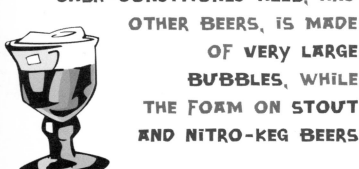

INCIDENTALLY, YOU WILL NOTICE
THAT THE FOAM ON
CASK-CONDITIONED ALES, AND
OTHER BEERS, IS MADE
OF VERY LARGE
BUBBLES, WHILE
THE FOAM ON STOUT
AND NITRO-KEG BEERS

IS MUCH FINER AND CREAMIER.
THE CLUE IS IN THE WORD
"NITRO-KEG". BIG BUBBLES
MEAN IT'S A CARBON-DIOXIDE
FOAM; TINY BUBBLES INDICATE
A NITROGEN FOAM.

FLOATING WIDGETS - TINY
HOLLOW SPHERES ABOUT THREE
CENTIMETRES (1.25 INCHES)
IN DIAMETER - IN CANS
OF BEER GENERATE A STREAM
OF NITROGEN WHEN THE CAN IS
OPENED TO CREATE A SMOOTH
NITROGEN FOAM, THUS IMITATING
THE HEAD CREATED WHEN
POURING DRAUGHT BEER.

FASCINATING, ISN'T IT?

When beers turn bad

BEER IS UNDOUBTEDLY MAN'S BEST friend, but there are a few occasions when it turns around and bites the hand that lifts it. Here are some symptoms of sick beer which are well worth looking out for.

The foam is "gushing".

IF YOU'RE HANDED A BEER THAT IS FROTHING OUT OF CONTROL, IT'S TOO WARM AND, THEREFORE, UNDRINKABLE. YOU MIGHT BE THE BIGGEST HEAD-CASE ON THE BLOCK, BUT YOUR BEER SHOULD NEVER LOOK LIKE VESUVIUS.

It tastes "cardboardy". It's stale and possibly oxidized. It might even taste a bit like sherry if this is the case. The beer is either past its sell-by date or it hasn't been stored properly (in a cool, dark place). There are certain full-flavoured beers, festival and seasonal ales, deep in colour and high in alcohol, that benefit from some ageing, but beer is generally best drunk fresh. How fresh is fresh? As a rule of thumb, cask-conditioned ales should be drunk within one month, keg beers within six weeks, while cans and bottles can gestate for up to nine months.

It looks hazy. Virtually every beer, with the exception of wheat beer, should be "bright". Haziness, which is derived from proteins in the malted barley, might also be another sign of staleness. Beer tends to get cloudier as it gets older.

My lager tastes "butterscotchy". The beer hasn't matured long enough.

It tastes "skunky" (as in like a skunk).

THE BEER IS "SUNSTRUCK", MEANING IT HAS REACTED BADLY TO LIGHT. BROWN GLASS FILTERS OUT MORE LIGHT, SO IT'S MORE PROTECTIVE THAN GREEN GLASS.

SOME PEOPLE, HOWEVER, SEEM TO PREFER THE FLAVOURS OF BEER BOTTLED IN GREEN GLASS. MAYBE IT REMINDS THEM OF A ROAD-TRIP OR SOMETHING...

While we're on the subject of bottles, some beer-drinkers swear blind that bottled beer tastes better and, specifically, less metallic than canned beer. The vast majority of beer cans are lined with an inert plasticky lacquer to prevent any contact with the can, so this is probably a psychological hurdle. Incidentally, when my fridge broke and decided to turn into a freezer, my canned beer froze solid, while the bottled stuff simply got colder. This could be useful information in the right hands.

But let's end on a happy note. My beer-boffin chum assured me that you'll never get food poisoning from beer, whatever might be wrong with it.

BEER IS TOO ACIDIC AND TOO HIGH IN ALCOHOL TO ALLOW ANY DISEASE-CARRYING MICRO-ORGANISMS TO SURVIVE. THERE IS ALSO VERY LITTLE

"FREE SUGAR" IN BEER FOR NASTY GERMS TO GROW ON, WHILE HOPS HAVE POWERFUL BACTERIA-KILLING PROPERTIES. SO, IF YOU'RE IN ANY DOUBT ABOUT THE LOCAL WATER, DRINK BEER.

Tasting beer: the language of love

swirl, sniff, & slurp - does your beer smell/taste:

Aromatic	spicy, vinous
Estery	banana, apple, candy
Fruity	lemon, apple, pear
Floral	rose, perfume
Resinous, grassy	fresh-cut grass, hay
Nutty	walnut, coconut, almond
Grainy	malt, straw
Roasted	caramel, liquorice, burnt, smoked, bread crust
Phenolic	tarry
Soapy, oily	cheesy, sweaty, buttery
Sulphury	struck match, rotten eggs, burnt rubber, cooked vegetables
Oxidized	stale, musty, catty, sherry-like, cardboardy, earthy
Sour	vinegary, like sour milk
Sweet	honeyed, vanilla-like, jammy
In terms of mouth-feel, is your beer:	soapy, creamy, metallic, dry, gassy, warming, watery, full-bodied, light-bodied

Mixing it: beer cocktails

YOU MIGHT THINK THAT MIXING good beer with anything is like drawing a moustache on the *Mona Lisa*, but even the most enigmatic of smiles can be improved with a nod and a wink. There's probably nothing I can say to persuade you to try any of these, but hey: maybe you were never bought a chemistry set as a kid, or maybe you'll just get bored one afternoon. Whether any of these combinations are better than the sum of their parts, only you can be the judge.

The classics

BRITS WILL HAVE HEARD OF THE FOLLOWING: SHANDY, WHICH IS BEER AND "LEMONADE" (A CARBONATED SOFT DRINK SORT OF LIKE SPRITE) OR BEER AND GINGER BEER – THE LAST WORD IN REFRESHMENT; BLACK VELVET,

WHICH IS STOUT AND CHAMPAGNE – THE LAST WORD IN SOPHISTICATION; AND SNAKEBITE, WHICH IS BEER AND CIDER – THE LAST WORD IN OBLIVION. BUT HAVE YOU HEARD OF THE FOLLOWING?

Hip & happening

In New York, the word on the street is that they're mixing beer with all sorts of spirits and fruit liqueurs these days (they just don't care, do they?). The "Michelada", allegedly from Mexico, is a glass of ice topped up with beer with the juice of one small lemon, a dash each of soy, Tabasco, and Worcestershire sauce, a pinch of salt and pepper, and, the *pièce de résistance*, a shot of Tequila.

Once you've cleared that one up you might want to try another NYC specialty, Raspberry Spiked Ale, which is a popular mix of beer with a dash of raspberry liqueur. Orange Spiked comes with a splash of Triple Sec, and Peach Spiked with Archers Schnapps.

Fruity tooty

Considering the awesome flavours of Belgian fruit beers, it shouldn't come as too great a surprise that beer and fruit can mix together rather well. The Germans, for example, are keen on adding a dash of raspberry cordial to tart wheat beers, while the Brits are partial to lager and lime and lager and black (blackcurrant).

Other beer-and-fruit combos, which I swear I haven't made up, include the Bee Sting (with orange juice), Isar Water (wheat beer with Blue Curaçao, orange juice, and apple juice), and the Liverpool Kiss, which is not a smack in the mouth but dark ale with cassis.

The Belgians, I am told, sometimes pep up their *frambozen* (raspberry beer) with a dash of Amaretto di Saronno almond liqueur.

Dark destroyers

The roasty, toasty flavours of stout seem to meld well with a range of tastes. The more traditional British drinks include Black Velvet (stout and Champagne) and Black and Tan (stout with bitter or mild). A Bourbon Black and Tan, surprisingly, comes with a dash of Bourbon. A poor man's Black Velvet is a Black Mambo (stout and cider), a variation on the Snakebite.

Alphonso Brown, the landlord of my favourite pub in Brixton, South London, told me that a half-and-half mix of stout and barley wine – which I can tell you is absolutely lethal – is called a Nigerian Lager. I've since learned that it's called a Blacksmith.

DRAGON'S BLOOD, BY THE WAY, IS BARLEY WINE WITH RUM, WHICH SOUNDS EVEN MORE DEADLY. A STOUT WITH WOODPECKER CIDER IS CALLED A BLACK PECKER, WHILE A STOUT WITH A GENEROUS SPLASH OF PORT IS A NICE, WARMING VELVET PUSSY. IF YOU'RE REALLY DESPERATE, A STOUT, CIDER, AND BLACKCURRANT IS CALLED A RED VELVET (PROBABLY BECAUSE YOU'RE LIKELY TO SPLASH THE CURTAINS.

Frisky with whisky

There's a natural affinity between beer and whisky, both of them being made from barley and all. If beer with a whisky chaser isn't cool enough for you, a Boilermaker is beer with a shot of whisky in it.

For the real psychos, a Depth Charge is beer with a shot of whisky in a glass at the bottom. The greater density of the whisky keeps it in the shot glass, releasing the perfect whisky kick as the beer glass is tilted, one sip at a time. It was probably invented by a desperate dentist, as the shot glass inevitably smacks you in the teeth with your last gulp. I once tried a cider Depth Charge (courtesy of Alphonso) with a glass of Drambuie at the bottom, but that's just plain silly…

Big in Japan

Beer and tomato juice, otherwise known as a Red Eye, is popular in downtown Tokyo, as is beer with cola, known as a Broadway. In the USA, the beer-and-tomato combo is called a Red Rooster or, with Tabasco added, a Ruddy Mary.

APPARENTLY, **ONE AMERICAN COLLEGE PARTY CLASSIC IS THE "SKIP AND GO NAKED".** THERE ARE HUNDREDS OF VARIATIONS - SOME STARTING, APPROPRIATELY ENOUGH, WITH THE WORD "HOP". ONE RECIPE CALLS FOR **BEER, LEMON JUICE, AND GIN** WITH A DASH OF GRENADINE FOR COLOUR, ALL MIXED TOGETHER IN A CLEAN GARBAGE CAN WITH A SKI POLE.

ENJOY!

BEER WITH FRIENDS

Beerheads

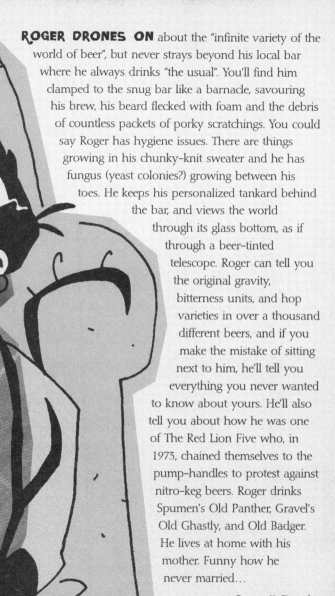

ROGER DRONES ON about the "infinite variety of the world of beer", but never strays beyond his local bar where he always drinks "the usual". You'll find him clamped to the snug bar like a barnacle, savouring his brew, his beard flecked with foam and the debris of countless packets of porky scratchings. You could say Roger has hygiene issues. There are things growing in his chunky-knit sweater and he has fungus (yeast colonies?) growing between his toes. He keeps his personalized tankard behind the bar, and views the world through its glass bottom, as if through a beer-tinted telescope. Roger can tell you the original gravity, bitterness units, and hop varieties in over a thousand different beers, and if you make the mistake of sitting next to him, he'll tell you everything you never wanted to know about yours. He'll also tell you about how he was one of The Red Lion Five who, in 1973, chained themselves to the pump-handles to protest against nitro-keg beers. Roger drinks Spumen's Old Panther, Gravel's Old Ghastly, and Old Badger. He lives at home with his mother. Funny how he never married…

2 Franck

FRANCK (PRONOUNCED FRAHNK) is from the Netherlands, and when he gets a little bit tipsy, he says he's "Amsterdamaged". He's a bit of a joker, you see. He owns one of those comedy baseball caps with the built-in beer receptacle with straws leading to his mouth. I know you've got one stashed away in the garage somewhere, but Franck actually *wears* his – along with his pencil-thin, piano-keyboard tie and novelty Scooby Doo socks. He also sports the killer "mullet" hairstyle and blond Tom Selleck moustache combo, unique to northern Europe. By day, he's a traffic warden – the cap looks wicked with his hairdo. But at the weekends Franck's "a real crazy party animal", playing keyboards in a Supertramp tribute band called Superdupertramp. When they're really rocking he punches the air and squeals like a distressed Bee Gee. Franck tried one of those home-brewing kits once, but his girlfriend threatened to throw him out when his flagon exploded all over her clean underwear. He drinks gallons of bland Eurofizz and puts mayo on his fries, but, hey: nobody's perfect.

3 Ken

KEN AND HIS BARBY (that's barbecue
to you and me) are inseparable. He might
think of himself as a laid-back beach bum,
but when it comes to burning flesh, he's
a charcoal Nazi. If you complain that your
sausage his raw in the middle, he'll call you
a wimp ("Botulism's a walk in the park
compared to some of the diseases I've beaten.").
If you're going to get on with chilled-out Ken,
the first rule you must learn is you *never* poke
another man's barby. And seeing that he's built like
the proverbial brick outhouse, you'd better listen.
For all his frazzled foodie pretensions, Ken refuses
to drink any beer you can actually taste – on principle.
He freezes his "tinnies" (cans to the rest of us) to the point
where your lips will get ice-burn unless you're careful,
but what do you expect from a man who
keeps bottles of Shiraz in the fridge? Always
prepared for an emergency, Ken has a
wall-mounted bottle opener in his camper
and wears a spare around his neck on a
piece of string. He's a keen surfer, so it's
ironic that, in beer terms, he's adrift in
a sea of gnats' pee. But you have to
admire the man's dentistry.

4 Denzil

KNOWN TO HIS FRIENDS AS "SPARKS",

Denzil hangs with the home boys in London's Notting Hill, and is what you might call a lager lothario. You'll find him getting down at DJ Norman Jay's red double-decker bus during the annual Carnival. He doesn't drink beer in industrial quantities, preferring alternative recreation, but when he does drink beer he goes for thick, malty brews you could stand a spoon in: beers with serious bass. Dragon Stout, which he swears "puts extra juice in his mango", is his top brew. But he doesn't drink it for his own gratification – oh no; he drinks it for the benefit of the "lay-dees". He also drinks a wicked mix of Guinness and barley wine, and the chicks don't seem to complain. Denzil spends ages on his mobile phone, saying "Yeah, sweet" a lot and instructing his bitches to "Come naked, bring beer." Once, when he was rapping into his phone, it rang back at him. Denzil's phone addiction is pretty surprising really, because when he's not chilling on the Hill, he works in telephone sales on a computer magazine.

5 Brett

BRETT IS AN ASPIRATIONAL BEER DRINKER
who'll drink anything the style mags tell him to. Anything
Japanese in a designer can will usually do the trick, or maybe an
unpronounceable Belgian fruit beer with a side dish of
pistachios. When he's dating, Brett will ostentatiously send back
at least one beer during the course of the evening. The bar staff
always look bemused, but they usually humour him. Brett
considers himself a bit of a metrosexual (an urban sophisticate
who isn't afraid of his feminine side). He wore a sarong in
Greece last year and is no stranger to body waxing, though he
drew the line at having a full "sack, back, and crack". Brett keeps
his terrifyingly tidy apartment well-stocked with the latest
gadgets. He was one of the first to buy a DVD player, when
even the most basic models cost over a grand. Well-done, Brett.
He compensates for his metrosexuality with false displays of
football/soccer fervour. He supported Manchester United a few
years ago, but now he's looking to quietly switch allegiance to
Arsenal without his buddies noticing. Fat chance.

Pub etiquette

4.2

BRITISH PUBS ARE TO BEER what cinemas are to movies: you can always rent a DVD, but it's not the same, is it? Where else but in a pub could you experience such a unique ambience, such fascinating behaviour, and such an intriguing range of smells?

BUT THE PUB CAN BE A HARSH, UNFORGIVING ENVIRONMENT IF YOU GET IT WRONG. SO, STUDY THIS COMPREHENSIVE CHECKLIST FOR SALOON-BAR SURVIVAL, AND FLUENCY IN PUB CULTURE WILL BE YOURS.

Getting a drink

Don't sit at a table expecting a waiter to glide up and take your order. It won't happen in a pub. There's nothing for it but to join the jostling throng at the bar.

WAVING CASH IN THE AIR IS VULGAR; EYE CONTACT IS BEST. I FIND A QUIZZICAL RAISING OF THE EYEBROWS

AND A SLIGHT, SUBSERVIENT, BACKWARD TILT OF THE HEAD (LIKE A REVERSE NOD) WORKS WELL. PRACTISE IN A MIRROR.

Never complain that you've been waiting for "half an hour". Everyone says this.

IF YOU THINK YOU'RE MAKING HEADWAY WITH THE BARMAID, DON'T OVERCOOK IT. WHEN SHE SAYS, "I BET YOU DON'T KNOW WHY THEY CALL ME Foxy," DO NOT REPLY, "IS IT BECAUSE YOU SMELL LIKE ONE?"

Ordering drinks

Britain's ancient licensing laws make it essential that ordering drinks is a smoothly run operation. If you're ordering a round (*see* below), do not order one drink at a time.

MAKE SURE YOU KNOW WHAT YOU WANT WHEN YOU EVENTUALLY GET SERVED. TRAIPSING BACK AND FORTH BETWEEN THE BAR AND YOUR TABLE TO FIND OUT IS NOT APPRECIATED.

LIKEWISE, DO NOT TAKE DRINKS BACK TO YOUR TABLE ONE AT A TIME AND STAY FOR A CHAT BEFORE PAYING. YOU WON'T MAKE ANY FRIENDS THIS WAY.

Do not order a pint of Guinness last as it takes a while to settle. And don't remind the bar staff to top it up. They know.

Don't wait until your round has been added up before asking about snacks. Do not ask the barperson to run through all the available flavours – twice – before deciding on plain crisps. And by the way, in Britain, potato chips are called "crisps". If you want fries, ask for "chips".

Paying

Pubs generally operate a simple pay-as-you-go system.
You will only be allowed to set up a tab under exceptional
circumstances – like if you risk ordering food.

YOUR CHANGE WILL NOT ARRIVE IN A LITTLE SILVER TRAY. YOU'LL BE PICKING IT OUT OF A PUDDLE OF BEER ON THE BAR.

NEVER DO THE "FUNKY WALLET DANCE": PATTING ALL YOUR POCKETS ONLY TO FIND, TRAGICALLY, YOU'VE LEFT YOUR WALLET AT HOME. IT'S JUST EMBARRASSING.

Buying rounds

When in groups, the Brits prefer to buy in "rounds".
It's so much more civilized than buying your own.
But remember, five people means five beers – or tears
before bedtime.

Consequently, "Fancy a quick pint after work?" is usually shorthand for "Let's get hammered". Under extenuating circumstances (i.e. it's Monday night), you could suggest everyone chips in to break this vicious cycle.

IF YOU ARE TRAPPED IN A ROUND SYSTEM, IT'S BEST TO STICK TO A "SESSION BEER" (LOW IN ALCOHOL) UNLESS YOU WANT THINGS TO GET MESSY.

In a rounds system, your drinking speed is conditioned by your associates. If you've already bought a round and you drink too fast, you either face a long wait for your next drink or you offer to buy an additional round, which seems a bit harsh. The third option is to buy a sneaky one and hide near the toilets while you drink it, but this is considered "bad form". If you haven't bought a round yet, drinking too slowly is absolutely no excuse for delaying your turn.

You can always buy yourself a half pint to allow your mates to catch up. But don't ask if anyone else would prefer a half. Complicated, isn't it? Being involved in a round is a gamble. Do you go first and buy for the group you're with, or do you delay and allow the round to get smaller – or bigger? Decisions, decisions…

Last orders

In England, we're proud to have the same licensing laws that were introduced in World War I to boost the war effort. You never know when you'll need them again, do you? And besides, nobody in Britain knows how to drink sensibly anyway. If you hear a bell at around 11 o'clock, it's not because there's a fire or to check you're still awake; It's to tell you to go home to bed. Do not wait for the lights to go off before ordering your last drink.

Beer olympics

You don't get to be great losers if you're not passionate about sports – and the Brits are great losers. Having said this, a lounge-bar lizard will not take kindly to being asked to move from his chair directly beneath the dartboard or next to the pool table unless a) there are plenty more spare chairs and tables available, or b) he's a lot smaller than you.

IF THEY'RE ALL SITTING IN A CIRCLE FACING YOU, THEY'RE NOT STARING AT YOU; THEY'RE TRYING TO WATCH A FOOTBALL/SOCCER MATCH, SO SIT DOWN!

There's no point trying to beat the world speed beer-drinking record, as the *Guinness Book of Records* has closed its data banks to any new entries. In case you're interested, Steven Petrosino drank one litre (35fl oz) of beer in 1.3 seconds on June 22, 1977, at the Gingerbread Man in Carlisle, Pennsylvania. A day that will live in infamy.

Pub quizzes help to maintain the social fabric of Britain, so it's considered very bad sportsmanship to use your mobile phone to call your buddy who's sitting in front of Google on his laptop.

IN THE LAVATORY NEVER OCCUPY THE MIDDLE URINAL IF THOSE ON EITHER SIDE ARE FREE. BREAKING WIND IS PERMITTED, WITHIN THE BOUNDS OF DECENCY, BUT FURTIVE SIDEWAYS GLANCING IS NOT.

LAUGH AT THE REALLY FUNNY ADVERTISING, USUALLY AT THE EXPENSE OF YOUR MANHOOD, CUNNINGLY PLACED AT EYE-LEVEL.

BEWARE HIGH-PRESSURE TAPS (FAUCETS) SHOULD YOU DECIDE TO WASH YOUR HANDS. "SPLASHBACK" IS A TERRIBLE THING.

IF YOU SHAKE IT MORE THAN TWICE, YOU'RE PLAYING WITH IT.

Playing top tunes

If you must play something by Justin or Britney, make it your last selection on the jukebox (is it still called a jukebox?) because, by then, you'll have vacated the area and no one will know you're responsible. Don't shout "Bo selecta!" when it comes on. You'll be made to feel like a puppy that's just crapped on the pub's sticky, swirly carpet.

If the pub is full of "grown men" crying into their beers, don't play "I Can't Keep My Eyes Off You" by the Pet Shop Boys.

If you're in any doubt, play "Eton Rifles" by The Jam ("Sup up your beer and collect your fags*"), "Born Slippy" by Orbital ("Singing lager, lager, lager, lager, lager, lager") or anything by The Clash, The Ramones, Dexy's Midnight

Runners, the Rolling Stones, Thin Lizzy or Toots and the
Maytals. It works for me.

* "fags": Britspeak for cigarettes.

Ordering food

There is a strange sub-sect of pub called "the gastropub"
where you can eat larks' tongue risotto in squid ink, but
the traditional boozer prides itself on indigestible snacks
in little bags (try the smoky bacon option and it will repeat
on you for days). My advice here is to treat anything in
a bar-mounted, heated display case with extreme caution,
if not downright suspicion. Arsenal Annie's assorted pies
are unlikely to be pushing the epicurean envelope.

Most pubs offer "specials" which are usually written on a
blackboard. Refrain from asking the bar staff to run through
them – twice – before opting for a bowl of chips (no; I'm
not going to explain it again; *see* "Ordering drinks", page 108).
Some pubs still offer free bar snacks such as roast potatoes,
pints of prawns or shrimps, and sandwiches. It is very bad
practice to abuse this goodwill gesture by "filling your boots".

Miscellaneous survival skills

If the Neanderthal next to you asks if you called his pint
a "poof" either a) explain carefully that you would
never call into question the sexuality of his chosen tipple,
or b) do a runner.

DO NOT MAKE FUN OF THE PERSONALIZED TANKARDS HANGING BEHIND THE BAR. ONE OF THEM PROBABLY BELONGS TO THE NEANDERTHAL NEXT TO YOU.

If a "dodgy geezer" (shady character) offers to sell you a DVD player on your way to the toilets, don't ask about warranties.

IF YOU HAVE YOUR GIRLFRIEND IN TOW, BUY HER A CHOCOLATE BEER AND THE BAR SNACK OF HER CHOICE. IT'S THE BEST WAY OF SAYING YOU'RE SORRY BEFORE YOU ACTUALLY HAVE TO.

5

UNDER THE INFLUENCE

5.1

A beer a day: beer & health

MEN'S HEALTH CONCERNS over beer-drinking are largely confined to the twin evils of beer bellies and "brewer's droop"; and the two are interconnected in the male psyche. We like drinking beer, we like having sex, but the gut gets in the way. "This isn't a beer gut, it's the fuel tank for a sex machine," announced a "comedy" T-shirt I spotted recently, summing up this curious combination of pride and shame in beer-assisted deformity.

NOW, I DON'T WANT YOU TO GET ALL EXCITED, BUT THERE IS COMPELLING EVIDENCE TO SHOW THAT THERE IS NOTHING INTRINSIC TO BEER THAT LEADS TO LAGER LOVE-HANDLES. THERE ARE ALSO ARGUMENTS - AND YOU'RE GOING TO LOVE THIS - THAT BEER COULD EVEN IMPROVE YOUR SEX LIFE.

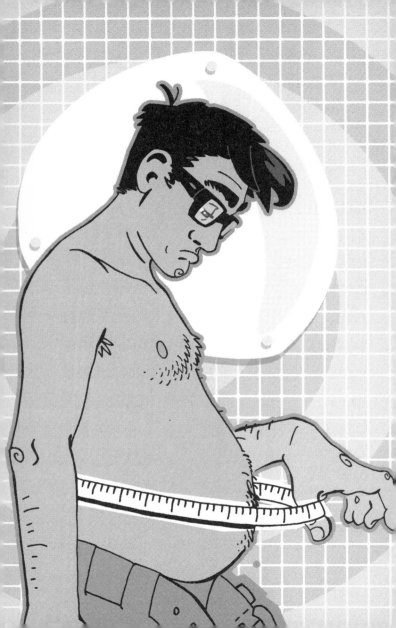

Turns out it's not a beer belly after all; it's a "lifestyle" belly. You in the back: stop giggling and listen to the facts. First off, let's compare beer with the "anti-beer": wine. According to the US Department of Agriculture Nutrient Data Laboratory, half a pint of beer at 4 degrees of alcohol contains ninety-one calories and nine grams of alcohol, while a 125ml (4fl oz) glass of wine at 12 degrees contains ninety-four calories and 11.9 grams of alcohol.

SO BEER CAN BE LESS FATTENING THAN WINE. IT ALSO CONTAINS LESS FREE SUGAR AND MORE DIETARY FIBRE (FROM THE BARLEY) AS WELL AS B VITAMINS, WHICH ARE NEGLIGIBLE IN WINE. WHAT'S MORE, BEER CONTAINS ALMOST NO FAT AND ZERO CHOLESTEROL.

Unlike wine, beer's very high water content (around ninety-three per cent) and its lower alcohol content make it a long, thirst-quenching drink that's very effective in countering dehydration. Low-alcohol beer has even been used as an isotonic sports drink in Germany, its readily available calories also providing a quick burst of energy.

SO HOW COME BEER SEEMS TO BE THE FAVOURED DRINK OF THE LARD-ASS? HOW DO I PUT THIS DELICATELY? IN ABSURDLY BROAD TERMS, BEER TENDS TO BE THE DRINK OF THE LOWER SOCIO-ECONOMIC CLASSES.

IN CONTRAST, STUDIES HAVE SHOWN THAT ASPIRATIONAL, LA-DI-DA WINE-DRINKERS TEND TO EAT MORE FRUIT AND VEGETABLES, LESS RED MEAT AND FRIED FOOD, AND THEY'RE LESS LIKELY TO SMOKE. IN SHORT, THEY'RE A BUNCH OF GIRLY WUSSES.

In scientific circles these other factors are called "confounders". And what confounds so many beer-drinkers is the extra-curricular eating that's so often accompanies a night out in the pub.

TAKE A DEEP BREATH AND COMPARE THE CALORIFIC CONTENT OF A LARGE GLASS (ABOUT 20FL OZ) OF BEER (ABOUT 185 CALORIES) WITH A 100G PACK OF PEANUTS (601 CALORIES, OR 3.2 GLASSES OF BEER), A QUARTER-POUNDER WITH FRIES ON THE WAY HOME (962 CALORIES, OR 5.2 GLASSES) OR CHICKEN CURRY WITH RICE (1,115 CALORIES, OR SIX GLASSES OF BEER).

DAMN THE CONFOUNDERS!

Another confounding nuisance for beer-drinkers is the pattern in which beer is often drunk: namely in a rounds system with friends. It's not *what* you drink, but *how* you drink it. Sensible drinking guidelines suggest that up to two large glasses (20 to 32fl oz) of beer a day is fine for most men. The tragedy is that you can't abstain all week and then go on a bender at the weekend. Sadly, it just doesn't work like that.

BUT IF YOU WANT TO DRINK SENSIBLY, IT'S MUCH EASIER TO KEEP TABS ON HOW MUCH ALCOHOL YOU'RE DRINKING WITH BEER THAN WITH WINE. IN BRITAIN, FOR EXAMPLE, A HALF-PINT (10FL OZ) OF BEER AT 4 DEGREES OF ALCOHOL EQUATES ALMOST EXACTLY WITH ONE UNIT OF THE BRITISH RECOMMENDED DAILY DOSE OF ALCOHOL.

You know where you are with a pint of beer, but a glass of wine can range from 125ml (4fl oz) at 11 degrees of alcohol up to 250ml (9fl oz) at a hefty 14 degrees. You do the math.

Mine's a large one

Another "humorous" beer T-shirt (they've got a lot to answer for) bears the legend: "Beer – helping ugly men have sex for 4,000 years." There is probably some truth in this, but, because heavy beer consumption can make a face like a bag of spanners look like Kylie Minogue, we should acknowledge that immoderate beer-drinking has, on occasion, landed us in deep doo-doo. Consider the wise words of UK rapper Mike Skinner: "I reckon you're an eight or a nine, maybe even a nine-and-a-half in four beers' time."

TOO MUCH BOOZE CAN MAKE A BUFFALO SEEM BEAUTIFUL, AND PROVIDE THE NECESSARY COURAGE TO OFFER IT FLOWERS AND CHOCOLATES. BUT (I AM TOLD) IT CAN ALSO LEAD TO LIMP DISAPPOINTMENT IN THE TROUSER DEPARTMENT, NOT TO MENTION THE PASSION-KILLING EFFECT OF TURNING UP ON YOUR GIRLFRIEND'S DOORSTEP, BURGER IN HAND, AFTER CLOSING TIME.

IN PARTS OF AFRICA AND THE CARIBBEAN, HOWEVER, IT'S THOUGHT THAT STOUT IS "GOOD FOR YOUR WOOD", THAT THERE'S "A BABY IN EVERY BOTTLE".

Supporting this theory, Dr Pavel Zemek of the Czech Centre for Gerontology in Prague argues that two beers a day can actually prevent impotence. He warns against excessive drinking, but says, "On the basis of clinical tests, we can say moderate amounts of beer lessens arterial sclerosis, one of the causes of erectile dysfunction."

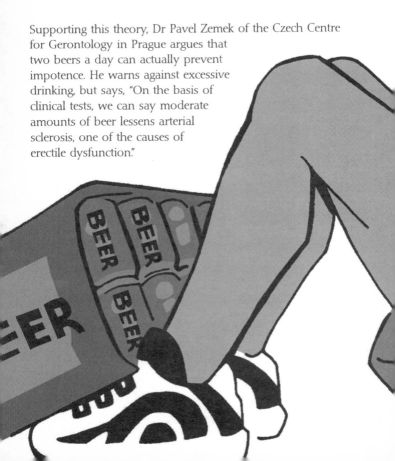

WHAT ZEMEK'S "CLINICAL TESTS" INVOLVED IS ANYONE'S GUESS, BUT THAT DOESN'T STOP YOU FROM ADDING "A BETTER SEX LIFE" TO YOUR LIST OF REASONS FOR GOING TO THE PUB. WATCH HER ARGUE WITH THAT ONE.

With regard to alcohol generally, numerous medical studies have shown that moderate drinkers are less prone to stress and heart disease than both teetotallers and heavy drinkers. Drinking alcohol in moderation can also strengthen your bones and reduce the likelihood of developing gallstones and kidney stones. Hops in beer, specifically, can help prevent dangerous blood clots.

SO, DITCH THE CIGARETTES
OR CIGARS, EAT SENSIBLY,
AND EXERCISE, AND THERE'S
ABSOLUTELY NO REASON WHY A
COUPLE OF BEERS A DAY CAN'T
FIT INTO A HEALTHY LIFESTYLE.

WHO KNOWS? WITH A LITTLE
EFFORT, YOU COULD EVEN
HAVE THAT WASHBOARD
STOMACH SHE'S BEEN DYING FOR,
INSTEAD OF THE TWIN-TUB
WASHER/DRYER YOU MIGHT HAVE
DEVELOPED OVER THE YEARS...

Ale & arty: beer with food

5.2

I FIND IT AMAZING HOW OFTEN BEER writers doff their caps to wine's perceived superiority. And I'm not at all surprised at how rarely the compliment is returned by wine writers. This is one of the only places you'll find wine mentioned in this beer book, and it isn't because beer is second-best when it comes to matching with food. Quite the reverse. There are loads of food matches where beer leaves wine floundering in its gorgeous, sparkling wake. And here they are.

Heat and spice and all things nice

Wine writers have been struggling for years to find wines that can stand up to Indian and Asian food. Just give up, guys; you'll never do it. Curry crucifies wine. It also needs a man's drink that can walk the walk in the company of chillies – and beer does it best.

BECAUSE OF ITS NATURAL SPARKLE AND STIMULATING BITTERNESS, BEER IS REFRESHING AND PALATE-CLEANSING IN WAYS THAT WINE CAN ONLY IMAGINE.

YES, I KNOW CHAMPAGNE IS SPARKLING, BUT HAVE YOU EVER TRIED IT WITH JALAPEÑOS?

Beer also has malty sweetness to balance heat, and much lower alcohol than wine, which helps to soothe a burning palate. Zippy pilsners and well-hopped beers such as India Pale Ale are particularly good at cutting through fats, oils, and heavy sauces. Ghee, the clarified butter in Indian dishes, and monosodium glutamate in Chinese food are simply brushed aside. Hops are also particularly compatible with the likes of cardamom and coriander. Effervescent wheat beers effortlessly slice through gloopy sauces, and their trademark banana and clove flavours resonate with Indian and Asian food.

SLIGHTLY SWEETER LAGER STYLES SUCH AS GERMAN DUNKEL AND FRENCH BIÈRES DE GARDE ARE WICKED WITH SWEET 'N' SOUR PORK AND CRISPY PEKING DUCK. AND BRING ON THE THAI, VIETNAMESE AND TEX-MEX, WHILE YOU'RE AT IT, BECAUSE THE SAME PRINCIPLES APPLY.

Food fit for heroes

Meaning fried chicken, pizza, cheeseburgers, bangers and mash (sausage and mashed potato), steak and fries, hot dogs, kebabs, burritos, salami, steak and kidney pie, and anything barbecued (even vegetables)... Need I go on?

THIS IS **NOT WHAT ARNOLD SCHWARZENEGGER WOULD CALL "GIRLIE FOOD". IT'S WHAT** I CALL **ROCK 'N' ROLL CAVEMAN COOKING, OR HPF (HEARTY PARTY FOOD).**

Girls have chocolate; we have the above – and it looks like a pretty good deal from where I'm sitting. Obviously, we couldn't survive or procreate the species on an exclusive diet of HPF, but, occasionally, we know we're worth it.

I COULD TELL YOU WHICH BEER GOES BEST WITH MELON, BUT IF YOU REALLY NEED THE ANSWER TO THAT, I THINK YOU'VE GOT A PROBLEM.

Here's some rocket science for you. Wine and beer deal in completely different flavours. While the grape and fruit flavours of wine can only provide contrasts with HPF, beer's bitter-sweet, roasted, caramelized repertoire brings perfect harmony.

THERE ISN'T A BEER INVENTED THAT CAN'T HUMBLE A SAUSAGE, AND BRITISH BITTERS IN PARTICULAR BRING "BANGERS AND MASH" TO THEIR KNEES.

DROWN BURGERS IN SWEET ONIONS AND MUSTARD AND, WHILE WINE WOULD RUN WEEPING TO THE SOMMELIER (WINE WAITER), IT'S NOT A PROBLEM FOR BEER.

While beer mixes and matches with HPF, its carbonation slices and dices through the fatty elements, refreshing the palate between each sinful mouthful. Check out the raisiny qualities of Trappist ales with crispy duck and game dishes; or the caramelized qualities of IPA, mild, old, and brown ales with spare ribs and roast chicken.

HOW ABOUT FRENCH BIÈRES DE GARDE WITH BEEF STEW; GERMAN HELLES AND DUNKEL BEERS WITH THE CRACKLING OF ROAST SUCKLING PIG; OR AMBER LAGERS SUCH AS MÄRZENBIER, OR MAYBE ALTBIER WITH THE YEASTY CRUST AND SWEET TOPPINGS OF A PIZZA?

Dark, roasted malts develop flavours of chocolate and coffee which marry perfectly with the charring on grilled foods and barbecues. And if you really want to send your barbecue into orbit, try some *Rauchbier* from Franconia, where the malt is smoked over beech wood (*Rauch* means smoke in German).

Fresh, hoppy pilsner, meanwhile, draws out the salt in bacon or smoked sausage and refreshes the palate beautifully.

For the ultimate in beer and meat harmony, sample a slice of *kobe* steak from Japan. These lucky cows are "fed" exclusively on beer and massaged with sake to make the most succulent and expensive steak known to man.

IF THE **ABOVE DIET** LEAVES YOU IN FEAR FOR YOUR LIFE, YOU COULD ALWAYS TRY A LIGHT, FRUITY, GOLDEN KÖLSCH WITH SALAD (IT WILL MAKE LIGHT OF A VINAIGRETTE DRESSING). OR MAYBE A SWEET, MALTY BOCK BEER WITH PUMPKIN RAVIOLI, OR ELSE A MALTY HELLES TO BRING SANITY TO THE NUTTY CHICKPEA FLAVOURS OF FELAFEL.

HAVE I CONVINCED YOU YET?

Fishing for condiments

Beer doesn't go with fish and seafood, does it? Well, think and drink again. The next time you drown your battered fish and chips in malt vinegar (or ketchup, if you must), remember that decent fish batter *contains* beer – and consider the obvious connections with the vinegar's malt. Also, bear in mind how well beer blasts through the mouth-coating

elements of this dish. I have even heard the theory that British bitter marries so well with fish and chips because much of it is made with maritime barley grown near the sea. I'll leave you to pick the bones out of that.

And what about that other British favourite: stout and oysters? This classic combination came about in the poor quarters of Victorian London but now graces any table. Stout also has a party with smoked fish like trout, salmon, and kippers, while the sweetness and caramelized flavours of seared scallops are a dream with sweeter porter.

Fizzy, citric wheat beer kicks ass with lobster, softshell crabs, spicy crab cakes and fried calamari, while the relatively acidic lambic beers of Belgium work a treat. The traditional Belgian dish of mussels steamed in *gueuze* is likely to make you very selfish with your shellfish.

The delicate flavours of shellfish shine clearly through pilsner, and who could resist a chilled jug of golden, foaming, hoppy lager with freshly barbequed sardines with olive oil and coarse sea salt? (You might want to check that you're not drooling all over the page at this point.)

Cheesy-peasy

Wine nerds share a deep, dark secret, but, under torture, they will confess that the marriage between red wine and cheese is a sham.

OFF-DRY WHITE WINES WORK BETTER WITH CHEESE – BUT BEER WORKS BETTER STILL. THE NUTTINESS AND SHARP ACIDITY OF MATURE CHEDDAR ARE PERFECTLY BALANCED BY THE BISCUITY MALT, BITTERNESS AND FRUITINESS OF A GREAT CASK-CONDITIONED ALE. AND IF YOU HAVEN'T TRIED IT, YOU SHOULD ENCOURAGE A SWEET, MALTY BARLEY WINE TO ELOPE

WITH A STRONG, SMELLY STILTON (OR OTHER BLUE CHEESE) FOR A UNION THAT IS TRULY BLESSED.

The French, who know a thing or two about cheese (and wine) know that their offensively smelly cheeses, like Münster, vacherin, and livarot, offer little resistance to a sturdy *bière de garde*, while the Belgians favour their sprightly lambic and fruit beers with tangy goats' cheese.

WINE FINDS IT DIFFICULT TO COPE WITH MOUTH-COATING FOODS SUCH AS CHEESE AND EGGS. PUT THEM TOGETHER IN EGGS BENEDICT OR A SIMPLE CHEESE OMELETTE AND WINE WILL REALLY SUFFER. A FRESH, ZIPPY WHEAT BEER, HOWEVER, WILL SPRING-CLEAN THE PALATE BETWEEN EACH MOUTHFUL, PLUMPING UP YOUR TONGUE

LIKE A SOFT FEATHER PILLOW
AND LEAVING YOU WANTING
MORE. MAKE IT YOUR NEW
BRUNCHTIME FRIEND.

Desserts: the pud, the bad, & the ugly

The "bad and the ugly" refers to chocolate, which is wine's worst nightmare. Even wine's greatest advocates have all but given up when it comes to the palate-polluting perils of the processed cocoa bean.

ONCE AGAIN, BEER'S
CARBONATION COMES TO THE
RESCUE, SCRUBBING UP YOUR
MOUTH FOR GREATER ENJOYMENT.

Death by Chocolate or hot fudge cake hold no fear for beers made with dark, roasted malts: stouts, porters, and, well, chocolate beers. And even the sweetest and messiest of chocolate frenzies cannot withstand the rich, raisiny charms of in-yer-face imperial stout.

BUT WHAT IF YOU'RE ON A DATE, AND YOU REALLY WANT TO IMPRESS YOUR LADY, WHO - AMAZINGLY - IS AS HAPPY DRINKING BEER AS YOU ARE? EASY. IF SHE ORDERS, SAY, CRÈME CARAMEL OR CRÈME BRÛLÉE, SUGGEST SHE TRY A SWEET, MALTY BOCK OR DIVINE TRAPPIST ALE TO GO WITH IT.

AND FRUIT DESSERTS? I HEAR YOU ASK. NO PROBS, BOB: A PLEASINGLY SHARP FRAMBOZEN WILL ALWAYS DELIVER THE GOODS, WHILE KRIEK WITH CHERRY CHEESECAKE IS A PARTNERSHIP SO PERFECT IT WILL LEAVE HER WEAK IN THE KNEES.

Don't beer afraid

The Belgians, French, and Germans are well-acquainted with the gastronomic pleasures of beer, and it's about time the rest of us took notice. There are some very encouraging signs, however, as beer lists are furtively nudging up against wine lists in a growing number of eateries. Even Gordon Ramsay's Aubergine restaurant in London has introduced a list of beers to match its Michelin-starred food.

Finding beer-and-food combinations is not like cracking a safe. The palate police won't come and laugh at you if you make an unconventional choice. And beer comes in tiny little bottles so you can afford to make a few pleasurable "mistakes".

SO... GET MIXING AND MATCHING, AND GET HAPPY!

Beer we go: beer festivals

5.3

THE WORLD IS AWASH WITH BEER
festivals, so here's just a taster of what's on offer. It could
make for a fascinating, beer-fuelled trip around the world,
with an awesomely busy September. But be warned: some
of these events are not staged every year and the dates
are subject to change, so please check the websites for
the latest information.

Miami Beach International World of Beer Festival
Miami, Florida, USA. January/February
www.worldofbeerfestival.com
Chill out on Miami's South Beach and soak up a "world-
class celebration of beer". Explore America's
micro-brewing revivalists. Don't forget to
roll up the sleeves on your pastel jacket.
Miami, nice.

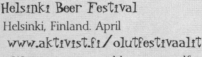

Helsinki Beer Festival
Helsinki, Finland. April
www.aktivist.fi/olutfestivaalit
Wrap up warm and have yourself a
drinky in Helsinki. The festival also
includes cider and whisk(e)y, which
makes for a potentially hazardous mix.

Australian International Beer Awards Festival

Melbourne, Australia. May
www.beerawards.com

Join the contestants to celebrate the bedrock of Australian civilization. The 2004 event received 885 entries from thirty countries. "It's all about the best beers in the world" according to the hype.

Belgian Beer Weekend

Brussels, Belgium. May
www.beerparadise.be

"Welcome to Belgian beer paradise" says the website, and who could argue with that? You will undoubtedly be spoiled for choice. Pack a reserve pair of adjustable-waistband trousers for *moules* and *frites* (mussels and french-fries) frenzies.

Le Mondial de la Bière

Montreal, Canada. June
www.festivalmondial
biere.qc.ca

Discover your inner lumberjack at this "brewing and culinary adventure". Try chocolate moose with your chocolate beer.

Darwin Beer Can Regatta

Darwin, Australia. July
www.ozoutback.com.au
Take part in the dancing and "unusual
contests" on Mindil Beach and make
yourself a boat out of beer cans.
Be sure they're empty first, though…

Great British Beer Festival

London, UK. August/September
www.gbbf.org.uk

Sup your way through the world's finest selection of
cask-conditioned ales at this CAMRA-organized event.
The excellent website has details of local UK beer
festivals, ranging from July's Devizes Beer
Festival in Wiltshire to the October
Festival in downtown Alloa,
Clackmannanshire.

Galway International Oyster Festival

Galway, Ireland. September
www.galwayoysterfest.com
There's a whole lot of shucking going
on at this Guinness-sponsored oyster
Olympics, and the pubs are alive with
the sound of music.

Stockholm Beer & Whisky Festival

Stockholm, Sweden. September
www.stockholmbeer.se

A smorgasbord of beer with whisk(e)y chasers and Bambi burgers all round. Swede dreams are made of this.

Great American Beer Festival

Denver, Colorado, USA. September/October
www.beertown.org

"Tour America's brewing landscape" with more than 1,500 beers from 300 US brewers. There is hope.

Oktoberfest

Munich, Germany. September/October
www.oktoberfest.de

The daddy of them all. Fill your boots with beer and your *Lederhosen* with sauerkraut at the world's most famous beer festival, where nearly eleven million pints of beer are drunk every year. Useful expression: *Bierdimpfe*, meaning "tavern potato".

Stuttgart Beer Festival

Stuttgart, Germany. September/October
www.wasen.de

The website recommends "the twenty-four-metre-high, colourfully decorated Fruit Column" in the festival grounds, a present from "the young and highly popular" Queen Katharina of Württemberg. Oh, and there's beer, too.

Bibliography

MICHAEL JACKSON'S BEER COMPANION
Mitchell Beazley, London, 1993

OLIVER GARRET THE BREWMASTER'S TABLE
Harper Collins, London, 2003

PROTZ ROGER THE ULTIMATE ENCYCLOPEDIA OF BEER
Prion, London, 1995

Acknowledgements many thanks to:

RUPERT PONSOBY AND ROSAMUND HITCHCOCK OF R&R TEAMWORK.

GABRIELLE ALLEN AND SARAH WYKES OF CARPE DIEM COMMUNICATIONS.

DR PAUL HEGARTY OF COORS' BEER NATURALLY CAMPAIGN